Holding On . . .
While Letting Go

Joan E. Hemenway

The Pilgrim Press
Cleveland, Ohio

The scripture quotations are from the Revised Standard Version of
the Bible, copyrighted 1946, 1952, © 1971, 1973 by the Division
of Christian Education of the National Council of the Churches of
Christ in the U.S.A., and are used by permission. The poems by R.L.
Sharpe and Angela Morgan are reprinted from *My Book of Prayers*,
copyright 1956, by permission of Fortress Press. The Hammarskjöld
prayer is reprinted from *Markings* by Dag Hammarskjöld, tr. Leif
Sjöberg and W.H. Auden, translation copyright © 1964 by Alfred
A. Knopf, Inc., and Faber and Faber, Ltd., by permission of Alfred
A. Knopf, Inc. The Gibran quotation is from *The Prophet* by Kahil
Gibran, renewal copyright 1951 by Administrators C.T.A. of Kahil
Gibran Estate, and Mary Gibran, and is used by permission of Alfred
A. Knopf, Inc.

Printed in the United States of America
05 04 03 02 01   12 11 10 9 8

ISBN 0-8298-0548-6

The Pilgrim Press, Cleveland, Ohio 44115

Preface

No one enjoys being in the hospital. It is an alien environment, a scary place filled with strange smells and sounds and people. We count the days, fear the pain, try to understand the diagnosis, are courageous in undergoing tests and treatments and examinations, welcome visits from family and friends—and most of all, wait expectantly to have it all over with and return home.

For more than ten years I have visited people in the hospital both as a hospital chaplain and as a local pastor. More recently I have been hospitalized myself. This experience has made me more aware of the gap between the hospital bed and the world, the sick and the healthy, being comforted and being the comforter. Support from family and friends, and professional help from doctors and nurses, are wonderful, necessary gifts in the face of illness and the threat of pain and even death. But when all is said and done, each person in the bed is finally left alone to withstand and understand the rigors of what is happening to body and soul.

The role of faith at such a time can be crucial, whether this is expressed in daily prayers and Bible reading, or simply in muffled, uncertain cries in the still of the night. God is listening for both, and more. How we make sense out of what is going on at such hard times is primarily the work of faith. And often it is the crisis of illness or unexpected tragedy that marks the real beginning of this work in our lives. For at such times we may be forced to wonder more deeply than ever before where God is, why this is happening to us, what we did wrong, why the world is so unfair, whether we will find strength to go on.

The prayers and poems and scripture readings in this book are ones I have found to be helpful both in my ministry and during my hospitalization. They are shared here in a spirit of openness and encouragement.

Come and be with me:

> All you who would believe but feel doubtful,
> All you who do believe and feel thankful,
> All you who want to believe and feel curious,
> All you who disbelieve but are not satisfied.

Holding On While Letting Go

When my young niece was learning to swim she never seemed quite able to let go. At first she always held on to me or the edge of the pool. As she got more sophisticated she was careful to keep the big toe of her right foot in contact with the bottom of the pool as she splashed vigorously on the top. I was not convinced, and she knew it!

Learning to swim is a lot like learning to have faith in a God who loves us but does not control or protect us. We are free to make our own mistakes, hold on to the sides when necessary, and even on occasion feel like we are drowning. Yet all the while we are surrounded by the waters of God's love, if we would but trust and let go. This is hard enough to do when everything is going smoothly, but in time of crisis it can be almost impossible. Sometimes I need a great deal more than one toe on the bottom to convince me that I won't drown. I am grateful that God's love does not depend on my faith!

My Daily Prayer

When we are scared, it is important to hang on to the sides. This prayer is one of my ways of doing this. Sometimes it even helps me to let go.

Almighty God, by whose will it is that we walk by faith and not by sight in the mysterious universe you have created: Increase now my faith in you, that in the midst of things which pass my understanding, I may not doubt your love, or miss your joy, or fail in my thanksgiving. Through Jesus Christ our Lord. Amen.

God's Promise to Us

These verses from the prophet Isaiah foretell the coming of the Savior, Jesus Christ. For me, they are broader than that, for I believe that we are each sent forth with a promise we will not return empty. This kind of purposefulness provides the framework for a faithful understanding of all that happens to us in a lifetime.

For as the rain and the snow come down from heaven,
    and return not thither but water the earth,
making it bring forth and sprout,
    giving seed to the sower and bread to the eater,
so shall my word be that goes forth from my mouth;
    it shall not return to me empty,
but it shall accomplish that which I purpose,
    and prosper in the thing for which I sent it.
                                        —Isaiah 55:10-11

A Prayer for Difficult Days

O God, some days are simply difficult. The breakfast is late, the doctor is early, visitors stay too long, flowers wilt, tests are not done, promises are broken, discouragement sets in. I know who I really am by how I respond to these frustrations and disappointments. Sometimes I am patient and can see beyond them. Sometimes they just do me in. Help me to be steadfast, O God, and hang in with both the good and the bad. Amen.

Stumbling Block or Steppingstone

Isn't it strange that princes and kings
And clowns that caper in sawdust rings,
And common people like you and me
Are builders for eternity!
Each is given a bag of tools,
A shapeless mass, a book of rules;
And each must make, e'er life is flown,
A stumbling block or a steppingstone.

—R.L. Sharpe

A New Sense of Peacefulness

Dear Lord and Father of mankind,
Forgive our foolish ways!
Reclothe us in our rightful mind,
In purer lives thy service find,
In deeper reverence, praise.

Drop thy still dews of quietness,
Till all our strivings cease;
Take from our souls the strain and stress,
And let our ordered lives confess
The beauty of thy peace.

Breathe through the heats of our desire
Thy coolness and thy balm
Let sense be dumb, let flesh retire;
Speak through the earthquake, wind, and fire,
O still, small voice of calm!
—John Greenleaf Whittier

A Benediction

May the strength of God guide us,
May the power of God preserve us,
May the wisdom of God instruct us,
May the hand of God protect us. Amen.

A Prayer About Friendship

Thank you, God, for all the friends who have reached out to me while I've been here in the hospital. Thank you for the cards and calls and flowers, for the gentle touch of hands and hearts and voices. They have helped me to feel alive and whole when I needed them most. They have helped me to find myself again. Thank you especially for the laughter and tears shared these past days, for our memories, and for all our hopes for one another. Bless my friends, O God, and keep them safe and close to you. Amen.

The Tie That Binds

Blest be the tie that binds
Our hearts in Christian love;
The fellowship of kindred minds
Is like to that above.

We share each other's woes,
Each other's burdens bear,
And often for each other flows
The sympathizing tear.

When we are called to part
It gives us inward pain,
But we shall still be joined in heart,
And hope to meet again.
—John Fawcett

Thoughts on Saying Grace

Bless, O God, this food to our use and us to thy service, and keep us mindful of the needs of others, for Christ's sake. Amen.

> Thou art great and thou art good,
> And we thank thee for this food;
> By thy hands will we be fed,
> Give us, Lord, our daily bread. Amen.

Some of the habits from our everyday routines can be carried over into our time in the hospital, when they may become newly meaningful. Saying grace at mealtime provides an opportunity to recognize God's gifts of daily sustenance at a time when we may be aware of how much we have been taking for granted. Sometimes saying grace with a chaplain or visitor can deepen our sense of connectedness and nurture, both physically and spiritually. Or saying grace silently and alone can act as a constant reminder that all we receive is given to us. And when we are not hungry but need to eat, saying grace can help us focus on the hard task ahead.

Coping with Anxiety

O God, there is so much to be anxious about in the hospital! Will I be all right? What will the doctors do? What if the nurses don't like me? I wonder if I'll ever get used to it here—this funny hospital gown, the hard bed, this fear of embarrassing myself, no snacks between meals, strangers who don't know me but are trying to help. O God, I am so uncomfortable. But you are my friend, my helper, my comforter. Be with me now and soothe my worries. Amen.

Therefore I tell you, do not be anxious about your life, what you shall eat or what you shall drink, nor about your body, what you shall put on. Is not life more than food, and the body more than clothing? . . . And which of you by being anxious can add one cubit to [your] span of life?

—Matthew 6:25, 27

A Truthful Word

Some of your hurts you have cured,
And the sharpest you still have survived,
But what torments of grief you endured
From evils that never arrived!
—Ralph Waldo Emerson

Prayer of Francis of Assisi

Lord, make me an instrument of your peace:
where there is hatred, let me sow love;
where there is injury, pardon;
where there is doubt, faith;
where there is despair, hope;
where there is darkness, light;
where there is sadness, joy.
Grant that I may not so much seek to be consoled as to
    console;
to be understood as to understand;
to be loved as to love;
for it is in giving that we receive;
it is in pardoning that we are pardoned;
and it is in dying that we are born to eternal life.
    Amen.

Praising God

Praise God from whom all blessings flow;
Praise God, all creatures here below;
Praise God with all the hosts above;
Praise God in wonder, joy, and love. Amen.

Thoughts on Confession

To make our confession means to draw near to God by coming clean and clear within ourselves. It means recognizing that we are human and not divine, fallible, needing to be forgiven. Confession is the path into deeper prayer. It involves a kind of intimacy and honesty that is hard, humbling, and well worth the effort. Dag Hammarskjöld expresses the essence of this movement within ourselves and toward God in this prayer:

> Give me a pure heart—that I may see Thee,
> A humble heart—that I may hear Thee,
> A heart of love—that I may serve Thee,
> A heart of faith—that I may abide in Thee.

Agnus Dei

O Christ, thou Lamb of God, that takest away the sin of the world, Have mercy upon us.

O Christ, thou Lamb of God, that takest away the sin of the world, Have mercy upon us.

O Christ, thou Lamb of God, that takest away the sin of the world, Grant us thy peace. Amen.

A Clean Heart

> Create in me a clean heart, O God,
>   and put a new and right spirit within me.
> Cast me not away from thy presence,
>   and take not thy holy Spirit from me.
> Restore me to the joy of thy salvation,
>   and uphold me with a willing spirit.
>   —Psalm 55:10-12

Amazing Grace

Amazing grace! How sweet the sound
That saved a wretch like me!
I once was lost, but now am found,
Was blind, but now I see.

'Twas grace that taught my heart to fear,
And grace my fears relieved;
How precious did that grace appear
The hour I first believed!

Through many dangers, toils, and snares
I have already come;
'Tis grace has brought me safe thus far,
And grace will lead me home.

When we've been there ten thousand years,
Bright shining as the sun,
We've no less days to sing God's praise
Than when we first begun.

Amazing grace! How sweet the sound
That saved a wretch like me!
I once was lost, but now am found,
Was blind, but now I see.

—John Newton

The Beatitudes

Blessed are the poor in spirit, for theirs is the kingdom of heaven.

Blessed are those who mourn, for they shall be comforted.

Blessed are the meek, for they shall inherit the earth.

Blessed are those who hunger and thirst for righteousness, for they shall be satisfied.

Blessed are the merciful, for they shall obtain mercy.

Blessed are the pure in heart, for they shall see God.

Blessed are the peacemakers, for they shall be called [children] of God.

Blessed are those who are persecuted for righteousness' sake, for theirs is the kingdom of heaven.

—Matthew 5:3-10

Sorrow

Who never broke with tears, his bread,
Who never watched through anguished hours
With weeping eyes, upon his bed,
He knows ye not, O Heavenly Powers.

—Goethe

A Prayer on a Dark Night

O God, I feel alone, frightened, angry. I'm afraid I won't get well. My body hurts all over, and my spirits are so low. I remember Jesus on the cross crying out, "My God, my God, why hast thou forsaken me [Matt. 27:46]?" I feel forsaken, but I don't want to give up. I feel so weak and tired and discouraged. The night is long and dark. Are you there?

Paul's Affirmation

But we have this treasure in earthen vessels, to show that the transcendent power belongs to God and not to us. We are afflicted in every way, but not crushed; perplexed, but not driven to despair; persecuted, but not forsaken; struck down, but not destroyed; always carrying in the body the death of Jesus, so that the life of Jesus may also be manifested in our bodies.

—2 Corinthians 4:7-10

A Psalm of Despair

I cry aloud to God,
aloud to God, that he may hear me.
In the day of my trouble I seek the Lord;
    in the night my hand is stretched out
        without wearying;
    my soul refuses to be comforted.
I think of God, and I moan;
    I meditate, and my spirit faints.
Thou dost hold my eyelids from closing;
    I am so troubled that I cannot speak.
I consider the days of old,
    I remember the years long ago.
I commune with my heart in the night;
    I meditate and search my spirit:
"Will the Lord spurn for ever,
    and never again be favorable?
Has his steadfast love for ever ceased?
    Are his promises at an end for all time?
Has God forgotten to be gracious?
    Has he in anger shut up his compassion?"
                                —Psalm 77:1-9

God's Mercy

But you are a chosen race, a royal priesthood, . . . God's own people, that you may declare the wonderful deeds of him who called you out of darkness into his marvelous light. Once you were no people but now you are God's people; once you had not received mercy but now you have received mercy.

—1 Peter 2:9-10

God's Faithfulness

I will never forget you, my people. I have carved you on the palm of my hand. I will never forget you; I will not leave you orphaned. I will never forget my own. Does a mother forget her baby? Or a woman the child in her womb? Yet even if these forget, yes even if these forget, I will never forget my own.

—Isaiah 49:14 ff., adapted

A Prayer Before an Operation

> God is our refuge and strength,
> a very present help in trouble.
> —Psalm 46:1

Dear God, be with me now as I wait and try to prepare for surgery. Help me to feel your caring embrace and be strengthened by your love for me. Be with the surgeon and the nurses and all who will take care of me in the days ahead. Help my family and friends to accept this time as necessary for me. I know there will be some pain and with your presence near me I will endure as best I can, knowing it will be good enough. Amen.

Watching and Waiting

> Out of the depths I cry to thee, O Lord!
> Lord, hear my voice!
> Let thy ears be attentive
> to the voice of my supplications!

*　　*　　*

> I wait for the Lord, my soul waits,
> and in his word I hope;
> my soul waits for the Lord
> more than watchmen for the morning,
> more than watchmen for the morning.
> —Psalm 130:1-2, 5-6

Prayer of Augustine

O Thou, from whom to be turned is to fall
    to whom to be turned is to rise
    and in whom to stand is to abide forever;
Grant us in all our duties thy help,
    in all our perplexities thy guidance,
    in all our dangers thy protection,
    and in all our sorrows thy peace.

A Song of Thanksgiving

Make a joyful noise to the Lord, all the lands!
    Serve the Lord with gladness!
    Come into his presence with singing!
Know that the Lord is God!
    It is he that made us, and we are his;
    we are his people, and the sheep of his pasture.
Enter into his gates with thanksgiving,
    and into his courts with praise!
    Give thanks to him, bless his name!
For the Lord is good;
    his steadfast love endures for ever,
    and his faithfulness to all generations.

—Psalm 100

If I Should Die

If it is now time, O God, let my spirit join with yours. My body is tired, and I know you have promised eternal rest. If I feel doubt and uncertainty, fill me with your love. If I fear entering the unknown, help me to trust in your goodness. I pray for my family and friends that they may not so much mourn my absence as celebrate the memory of my presence and rejoice in my living. If I am to enter a new time and a new journey, I ask for peace, O God, and a deepening sense of your mighty grasp of me. Amen.

Eternal Life

Only when you drink from the river of silence
    shall you indeed sing.
And when you have reached the mountain top,
    then you shall begin to climb.
And when the earth shall claim your limbs,
    then shall you truly dance.

—Kahlil Gibran

A Blessing

Now unto the one who is able to keep us from falling and to present us faultless before the presence of glory with exceeding joy, to the only wise God, our Savior, be glory and majesty, dominion and power, both now and forevermore. Amen.

—Jude 24-25, adapted

The Shepherd Hymn

Psalm 23 is perhaps the best known and most loved psalm of all. There are a few paraphrases and this is one of my favorites in the form of a hymn.

The king of love my shepherd is,
Whose goodness faileth never;
I nothing lack if I am his,
And he is mine forever.

Where streams of living water flow,
My ransomed soul he leadeth,
And where the verdant pastures grow,
With food celestial feedeth.

Perverse and foolish oft I strayed,
But yet in love he sought me,
And on his shoulder gently laid,
And home, rejoicing, brought me.

In death's dark vale I fear no ill
With thee, dear Lord, beside me;
Thy rod and staff my comfort still,
Thy cross before to guide me.

Thou spread'st a table in my sight;
Thy unction grace bestoweth;
And O what transport of delight
From thy pure chalice floweth!

And so through all the length of days
Thy goodness faileth never;
Good Shepherd, may I sing thy praise
Within thy house forever.

—Henry W. Baker

The Bread We Need

Oftentimes new words can bring new life to our old, familiar prayers and ways of praying. Jesus said, "And when you pray, you must not be like the hypocrites; for they love to stand and pray in the synagogues and at the street corners, that they may be seen. . . . Truly, I say to you, they have received their reward. But when you pray, go into your room and shut the door and pray to your Father who is in secret; and your Father who sees in secret will reward you [Matt. 6:5-6]." A hospital stay can be a perfect time to go into that secret place of prayer, perhaps with some new words, and find the bread you need.

The Lord's Prayer

Our God, holy be your name,
Your kingdom come, your will be done
on earth as in heaven.
Give us today the bread we need.
Forgive us our sins
as we forgive those who sin against us.
Save us in the time of trial,
and deliver us from evil.
For the kingdom, the power, and the glory
are yours, now and forever. Amen.

A Prayer for the End of the Day

O Lord, support us all the day long, until the shadows lengthen and the evening comes, and the busy world is hushed and the fever of life is over, and our work is done. Then in thy mercy grant us a safe lodging and a holy rest and peace at the last. Amen.

—John Henry Newman

God's Glory and Mine

I am aware, as I go commonly sweeping the stair,
Doing my part in the every day task,
I am aware of the glory that runs
From the core of myself to the core of the suns.
Bound to the stars with invisible chains.
Blaze of eternity now in my veins.

—Angela Morgan

Keeping Faith

We are simply asked to make gentle our bruised
    world,
to tame its savageness,
to be compassionate to all, including ourselves,
and then, in the time left over,
to repeat the ancient tale
and go the way of God's foolish ones.

Going Forth

Go forth in peace; be of good courage;
Hold onto that which is good;
Return no one evil for evil;
Strengthen the fainthearted;
Support the weak;
Help the suffering;
Honor all people;
Love and serve the Lord,
Rejoicing in the power of the Holy Spirit. Amen.